Dedicated to all dog lovers, to friends of Moe
and to those who strive to live their best each day.

Special thanks to Dr. Aliya Magee and LSU School of
Veterinary Medicine for their extraordinary care;
Kaela Massey, Carla Crooks, and Deb Erickson
for their priceless input.

FIRST EDITION
Published by Play Tall LLC
Edited by Margaret Civella; iReview Content Marketing and Publishing

Miracle of Moe

Written by Patsy Burdine

Illustrated by Brian Oakley

Moe is an ordinary little dog who was born with lots of other puppies. Mr. Luis & Ms. Patty love their dogs so much, especially all the new ones.

Ms. Patty feeds and plays with them and gives them soft toys to snuggle with. They raise all their puppies until they grow big enough to find their perfect home with their new families.

One day a very nice couple came to see Moe. They seemed to like him a lot and decided he would be perfect for their home.

Moe was very happy to have a new home and family of his own. How exciting to have a sister. Her name was Stella and she was super outgoing, really fun and very, very fast.

Moe was fitting into his new home very well. Mom liked to give them baths and brush their hair.

While he liked getting all the attention with suds and scrubs, what he liked most...was the hair dryer.

He loved the warm air blowing dry his black and brown fur.

One day Mom took Moe and Stella to the doctor for a checkup. He liked this place called LSU. They take care of every kind of animal you can think of.

Moe saw little cats and big horses.
There was a screech owl and a brown pelican...
even a baby zebra.

He met so many new friends.

Dr. Magee was Moe's doctor. She was very nice and very pretty. She liked Moe a lot but had some bad news.

Moe had a terrible problem with his heart and she wasn't sure he would live much longer, which made Moe's parents very sad.

Dr. Magee also had good news. She had medicine for him. So she gave him his medicine and a kiss on the head and off they went back home.

Moe continued to take his medicine and see his doctor. To everyone's surprise he grew bigger every day. He ran and played with Stella.

She taught him how to guard the yard, bark at the mailman, play with toys and chew on bones. He learned quickly and gained energy.

His mommy called him a Miracle.

Moe continues to live his best every day and doesn't let anything get in his way.

He wakes up happy enjoying whatever life brings, finding the joy in every moment. He found that choosing to be happy is much more fun than being sad or mad.

And Moe is up for any new adventure, his very, very favorite is riding a bike.

He also learned that being cute has lots of benefits. He gets all the attention, lots and lots of toys, extra hugs and more cookies.

Just being himself is the best trick he knows.

And Moe is kind to others. He always has a smile and a wiggle for them and it seems to make their day better. Being kind to others never hurts him and always seems to help them.

Moe loves with all his heart. Even the hard to love people. Sometimes they disappoint him, but he never regrets loving them anyway.

And....

Moe learned to never pass up the chance for a nap.

Moe is special.

Moe is a Miracle.

Visit our facebook page at
www.facebook.com/Miracle Of Moe
and look for more books and blogs from Moe.

For more copies of Miracle of Moe,
visit www.patsyburdine.com/miracleofmoe

This short little story was written about a
short little dog with a very big heart...literally.
Moe has a heart defect called subaortic stenosis.
It is severe enough that it cannot be fixed with surgery.
Moe's heart has to work much harder to do the same job
as other pets or people, so his heart becomes enlarged,
leading to a much shorter life span.

None of us know how many days we have and neither does Moe.
He simply lives his best every day. Oh, if we could only do the same.
All our lives are miracles. Live your best life today!

~ Patsy Burdine

A portion of the royalties from the sale of *Miracle of Moe* will be donated to
the LSU School of Veterinary Medicine.